TIME TRAVELING TO
1982

RELIVING A VERY SPECIAL YEAR

TIME TRAVELING TO 1982

Author
Duncan L. Hayward

Design
Gonçalo Sousa

June 2022

ISBN: 9798833016916

Reliving the culture, the people, the World events and the art that made 1982 a magnificent year!

Contents

Chapter Six: Births And Deaths 1982

Chapter Seven: Statistics 1982

Chapter One: News & Current Events 1982

Leading Events

January 18th-April 22nd: Carlos 'The Jackal' Terrorist Attacks

Carlos The Jackal (Ilich Ramírez Sánchez) was a high-profile terrorist who was responsible for a multitude of terrorist attacks and bombings during the Seventies and Eighties. His terrorist group's first attack in 1982 was on January 18th, when they attempted to blow up the Superphénix Nuclear Power Station in Creys-Malville, France. A number of rockets were fired, but the attack was unsuccessful. On February 16th, two of his group's members - Bruno Breguet and Sánchez's then-girlfriend (some reports say she was his wife),

Venezuelan terrorist
Ilich Ramirez Sanchez,
also known as Carlos the Jackal

Magdalena Kopp - were arrested in Paris. Sánchez launched a series of attacks in reprisal. The first was on March 29th with the bombing of the Paris-Toulouse TVG train that killed 5 people and injured 28 (some reports state 77) (France24.com). Nearly a

Superphénix nuclear power plant, Isere, France

month later, on April 22nd, Sánchez was involved in the Paris Rue Marbeuf car bombing that targeted the headquarters of the anti-Syrian newspaper Al-Watan Al-Arabi. The explosion killed one person and wounded at least 60 others (France24.com). Sánchez was eventually caught in August 1994 and is currently serving three life sentences.

April 2nd-June 20th: Falklands War

The Falklands War officially started on April 2nd when invading Argentinian troops overpowered the limited British military presence in the capital Port Stanley (approximately 70 poorly-equipped Royal Marines that made up Naval Party 8901); despite a valiant stand from NP8901 against massive odds, it was achieved without any loss of British life. The British response was swift, and on April 5th, a 100-ship task force was dispatched to begin the process of retaking the islands. There were many key moments during the conflict. One such event was the sinking of the A.R.A. General Belgrano cruiser,

British military people of the Falklands War

which was just outside the 200-mile exclusion zone, by the British submarine H.M.S. Conqueror on May 2nd. This resulted in the deaths of over 300 Argentinian crewmembers. Just two days later, on May 4th, H.M.S. Sheffield was hit by an Exocet missile and sank with 20 British sailors killed. Other vessels that were sunk included H.M.S. Antelope (May 23rd: 2 dead), H.M.S. Coventry (May 25th,

Exocet - 19 dead), S.S. Atlantic Conveyor (May 25th, Exocet, sunk - 12 dead), and R.F.A. Sir Galahad (June 8th - 48 dead/115 wounded) (Naval-History.net). Toward the end of the conflict, there were a number of ferocious clashes on land, such as the Darwin/Goose Green assault, and the battles for Mount Longdon, the Two Sisters, Mount Tumbledown, Wireless Ridge, and Mount Williams. Rather than engage in a hopeless battle to retain Port Stanley, which would have resulted in serious civilian casualties, the Argentinian commander, Brigadier General Mario Benjamín Menéndez, was

persuaded to surrender on June 14th and the Falklands War was over. Coming full circle, it was the members of NP8901, who had returned to fight after being flown home following their capture, that once again raised the British flag outside Government House.

British war graves, Falkland Islands 1982

April 27th-June 21st: Trial Of John W. Hinckley, Jr.

John Warnock Hinckley, Jr. attempted to assassinate the 40th President Of The United States, Ronald Wilson Reagan, on March 30th, 1981. President Reagan had just finished attending an A.F.L.-C.I.O. (American Federation Of Labor And Congress Of Industrial Organizations) meeting at the Washington Hilton Hotel. As he made his way toward his limousine, he was shot by Hinckley, Jr. The would-be assassin fired six shots from a Röhm RG-14 .22 caliber gun; initial shots missed, but the sixth and final shot eventually hit

President Reagan after it initially
bounced off the armored limousine. The
President was rushed to George
Washington University Hospital, where
President Reagan actually insisted on
walking into the hospital. President
Reagan was in surgery for a couple of
hours, already back to work and signing
documents the next day, and eventually
returned to the White House on April
11th. Hinckley, Jr. was indicted on 13

Hinckley on March 30, 1981
the day of the shooting

charges, including attempting to kill President Reagan, and his trial
started on April 27th, 1982. Following an eight-week trial, the jury

Ronald Reagan was shot by John Hinckley Jr.

found him not guilty on
any of the 13 counts due to
insanity. He was still
considered dangerous
despite the verdict, and
John Hinckley, Jr. was sent
to St. Elizabeth's Hospital
in Washington, D.C. He
remained there until 2016,
when he was given a
conditional release.

June 3rd-September 29th: Lebanon War

On June 3rd, Shlomo Argov, the Israeli Ambassador to Britain, was
shot in the head with a Polish WZ-63 machine pistol by Hussein
Ghassan Said as he left a function at the Dorchester Hotel in
Mayfair. Ghassan Said fled the scene, but was swiftly caught and also

shot in the head by Argov's
bodyguard, Colin
Simpson. Surprisingly,
both men survived their
wounds. The next day,
Israeli Prime Minister,
Menachem Begin, declared
that the assassination
attempt was an attack on
the state of Israel and
ordered strikes on

Navy fighters and the Paratroopers
Brigade on a voyage

Palestine Liberation Organization targets in Lebanon. In retaliation,
the P.L.O. launched rockets, mortars, and artillery of their own on
the Galilee area of Israel. Just a couple of days later, on June 6th, the
Israeli Defense Forces began "Operation Peace For Galilee." The
objectives of the operation were to destroy P.L.O. bases and terrorist

Paratroopers in Lebanon

infrastructure, to remove
the P.L.O. from Lebanon,
and ultimately remove any
military threat to
Northern Israel. The
initial plan involved a 25-
mile/40-kilometer sweep
across Southern Lebanon,
but the I.D.F. swiftly

achieved that goal and continued northward, quickly reaching Beirut
by June 9th. With the now expanded intention to remove the P.L.O.
from Beirut, the Israeli forces attacked and besieged the capital city
of Lebanon. Despite the occasional unsuccessful ceasefire, the war
around Beirut raged for many weeks, with casualties on all sides,

including civilians. On August 21st, French, American, and Italian troops arrived to assist with the agreed removal of P.L.O. forces from Beirut. The end of this particular Middle East conflict came on September 29th, when the majority of Israeli forces withdrew from West Beirut.

Other Major Events

Multiple Dates In 1982: Northern Ireland Troubles Continue

The Northern Ireland Troubles continued to be a part of the news, and the Provisional Irish Republican Army carried out multiple bombings throughout this year. A series of explosions in Northern Ireland occurred on April 20th. Two people (Wilbert Kennedy and Noel McCulloch) were killed when a bomb exploded at the Diamond, Magherafelt, County Derry. On the same day, a further 12 people were injured in blasts that took place in Armagh, Ballymena, Belfast, Bessbrook, and Derry.

Belfast IRA men with a drogue bomb in 1982

An army captain being rescued after being heavily stoned and kicked

Just three months later (July 20th), the Provisional I.R.A. was responsible for two bombs that exploded in London near Hyde Park (South Carriage) and Regent's Park (bandstand); 11 British Army personnel (4 Hyde Park, 7 Regents Park) and 7 military horses were killed, and 47 civilians (23 Hyde Park, 24 Regents Park) were also injured (Cain.Ulster.ac.uk). The other notable incident in 1982 was the Droppin' Well Bar bombing in Londonderry on December 6th, when the Irish National Liberation Army detonated a bomb that killed 11 British soldiers and 6 civilians; another 30 civilians were also injured.

October 11th: Mary Rose Raised From The Solent

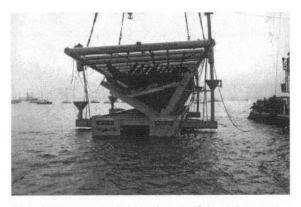

The final stages of the salvage of the 16th century carrack Mary Rose on October 11, 1982

An item of English historical significance saw the light of day for the first time in 437 years in October. Built between 1509 and 1511, the Mary Rose, the flagship of Henry VIII, had served as part of the King's Navy for 33 years until she sank on July 19th, 1545. Lost to the sediment of The Solent, she was rediscovered on May 5th, 1971. Many excavations were carried out, and the Mary Rose Trust was formed in 1979. The decision was eventually made to raise the main hull of the wreck using a steel lifting frame and steel cradle. The operation cost £4 million and was postponed twice due to bad weather, but on October 11th, the Mary Rose was raised from the water. The event was watched by an estimated 60 million people worldwide in the first-ever live underwater broadcast, and the Mary Rose now rests on display at the Portsmouth Historic Dockyard.

Political Events

January-November: U.S. Recession

The U.S. economy officially entered into a recession during the third quarter of 1981 (July) and it lasted until the last quarter of 1982 (November). America had already just experienced a recession that was caused by the 1979 oil price shock and inflation growing to 13.5%. At 6 months, it was tied for the shortest

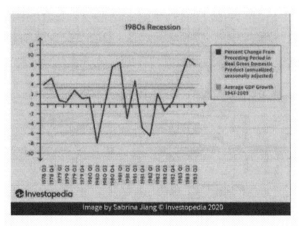

The short recession at the start of the decade and the following brief period of growth, as well as the deeper recession in 1981 and 1982 have led to the period being characterized as a W-shaped recession

post-W.W.II recession on record. Unfortunately, optimism didn't last, and the United States quickly experienced a second recession just weeks later, a double-dip recession that was much harsher than its predecessor. Interest rates reached 21.5%, unemployment grew from 7.4% to around 10%, and the economy declined by 3.6%. By October 1982, inflation was at 5%, interest rates at 9%, and unemployment at 8% (FederalReserveHistory.org).

April 17th: Signing Of Canadian Proclamation Of The Constitution Act

The Canadian Proclamation Of The Constitution Act was signed on April 17th by H.R.H. Queen Elizabeth II and Canadian Prime

Minister Pierre Trudeau in Parliament Hill, Ottawa. By the early 1980s, Canada already had many aspects of a nation that was both sovereign and independent, but it was unable to amend its own constitution without permission from Great Britain. Despite Britain having agreed to

Her Majesty Queen Elizabeth II with Prime Minister The Rt. Hon. Pierre Elliott Trudeau signing the Constitution

grant autonomy to most of its previous empire, there had always been an argument within Canadian politics as to how this could be achieved and the mechanisms for making constitutional changes. In November 1981, Prime Minister Trudeau was eventually able to achieve agreement between the government and all but one of the ten provinces (Quebec) on a constitutional proposal to be submitted to Great Britain; it also included a Charter of Freedoms and Rights. The British Parliament approved the Canada Act (Constitution Act

Of 1982) on March 25th, and the signing on April 17th between the two Heads Of State granted Canada its complete independence.

Proclamation of the Constitution Act, 1982

July 23rd: International Whaling Commission Commercial Whaling Ban

At the 1982 International Whaling Commission meeting held in Brighton, the sixth item on the agenda was the discussion about a proposal from five countries (Seychelles, U.K., U.S.A., France, and

Whalers illegally hunted thousands and thousands of whales

Australia) that sought an end to commercial whaling. The proposal was approved by a majority with 25 votes in favor, 7 against, and 5 abstentions (WWF.Panda.org). The agreement was to bring in a moratorium on all commercial whale hunting that would begin in 1986. The ban continues to this day and has generally been considered a success.

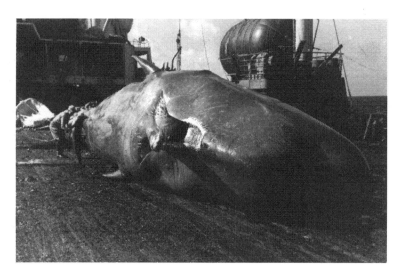

The Soviets hunted sperm whales mostly for their oil, which was valuable as an industrial lubricant

28th October: Population Of China Reaches One Billion

On 28th October, China reported that its population had surpassed 1 billion for the first time. The figure had grown by almost 50% in 18 years, with the actual number quoted at 1,008,175,288 (WashingtonPost.com). It amounted to approximately one-quarter of the planet's total population.

Street in China, 1982

Other Notable Events

January 13th: Air Florida Flight 90 Crash

The intended destination for Air Florida Flight 90, a Boeing 737-222, was Ft. Lauderdale-Hollywood International Airport. However, the take-off was delayed by 1 hour and 45 minutes due to heavy snowfall that forced Washington National Airport to temporarily

Navy divers load a recovered piece of the landing gear from Flight 90

close. When it finally reopened, the plane was de-iced as usual, but ice made it difficult to move the plane to the runway. The flight's departure was again delayed for another 45 minutes before take-off clearance was finally granted. Not only was the plane not de-iced again, but the crew failed to turn on the anti-ice systems. Ice had reformed on the wings, and the lack of anti-ice mechanisms provided engine thrust readings that were higher than they actually were. The plane took off at 15.59, but the lack of propulsion due to incorrect readings meant it was only able to achieve a few hundred feet of altitude. Air Florida Flight 90 crashed into the 14th Street Bridge about 30 seconds later, then fell into the freezing Potomac River. The plane took off with 74 passengers and 5 crew. It was concluded that 73 passengers died on impact, and a further four motorists were killed. Four passengers and one attendant survived the crash. Arland Williams was one of the six who actually escaped, but in an act of extreme heroism, he continually passed the rescue rope from the only rescue helicopter that could attend the scene to others and drowned in the process. The 14th Street Bridge was eventually renamed the Arland D. Williams, Jr. Memorial Bridge in recognition of his actions.

Navy divers watch as a crane lifts a load of wreckage from Flight 90

June 21st: Birth Of Prince William

Prince William Arthur Philip Louis, the future King of the United Kingdom and Commonwealth, was born at 21:03 on June 21st. He was born at St. Mary's Hospital in London and was the first member of the Royal Family to be born in a hospital. Princess Diana was in labor for approximately 16 hours, but Prince William, now The Duke Of Cambridge, was delivered safely, weighing a healthy 7lb 1oz.

A son for Princess: 7lb baby and mother doing well

21st June 1982 – Birth of Prince William

October 1st: Disney Opens EPCOT Center

Walt Disney World in Florida officially opened on October 1st, 1971, with the main attraction being the Magic Kingdom theme park. The second major part of Walt Disney World opened to the public on October 1st, 1982. The EPCOT Center (Experimental Prototype Community Of

Spaceship Earth, Epcot

Tomorrow) was one of Walt Disney's last major ambitions. His intentions for building Walt Disney World/The Magic Kingdom were, at least in part, to aid with the financing of the EPCOT Center. His vision was to create an actual city where people worked, lived, and played, but he passed away in 1966, long before his vision could be refined or realized. The executives in charge felt that it was an uncertain project without Walt Disney's personal vision, but, eventually, the idea was given another chance. The ground for the EPCOT Center was broken on October 1st, 1979, with the finished park opening just two years later.

Chapter Two: Crime & Punishment 1982

Major Crime Events

June 17th-June 28th: Barry Prudom Murders and Manhunt

Barry Peter Prudom, who was also known as The Phantom of The Forest, was a multiple murderer who was the focus of the largest armed police operation in Great Britain, involving 12 different police forces. On June 17th, Police Constable David Haigh was found dead next to his car after failing to respond to his radio; he had been shot once in the head. Prudom broke into the house of Freda Jackson on June 20th, stole £4.50, and

Barry Prudom

left her tied up. He then broke into the house of George and Sylvia Luckett in the early hours of June 23rd. He tied both up, shot them in the head (killing George, but Sylvia survived), and stole their car. During a routine stop on June 24th, he fired several shots at P.C. Kenneth Oliver, one of which hit him in the face, but he was able to escape

Prudom's killing spree sparked a huge police manhunt

15

when the officer's dog attacked Prudom; he also shot the dog, but both officer and dog survived. He then fled into Dalby Forest and avoided capture, despite a manhunt comprising 1,000 officers and helicopters. Prudom had been identified by June 28th, and, responding to a call about a suspicious man, Police Sergeant David Winter and P.C. Mick Wood encountered Prudom. The fugitive fired three shots and killed Winter. Prudom was eventually tracked down in Malton and surrounded. When a shot was heard, the firearms squad opened fire, and Prudom was later found dead. Despite 21 wounds, it was determined he killed himself with a bullet to the head.

July 9th: Michael Fagan Break-In at Buckingham Palace

Michael Fagan became notorious in 1982 when he managed to break into Buckingham Palace. Fagan claimed that he actually broke into the Palace twice. On June 7th, he said he was able to get into the Palace through an unlocked window before strolling around as he ate crackers and cheese. He tripped alarms, but this was ignored as the staff assumed it was a false alarm. Fagan claimed that he'd sat

Michael Fagan

on the throne, looked at all the portraits, and even had time to drink a bottle of wine before exiting the building without being discovered. Around a month later, Fagan did it again. At approximately 07:00 on July 9th, Fagan climbed the walls and then made his way up a drainpipe, and once again entered through an unlocked window. Although he tripped alarms again, this was also put down to false sensor readings. Fagan was able to make his way into the Queen's bedroom. He pulled back the curtains to find H.R.H. Queen Elizabeth II asleep in bed and woke the startled British Monarch. Accounts vary as to what happened next, but it would appear that the Queen tried unsuccessfully to call security via the night alarm button and then phoned the police. After they didn't arrive quickly enough, Fagan claimed she climbed out of bed and found a footman, Paul Whybrew, and a maid. They both kept Fagan in the pantry until the police arrived. Trespassing was a civil matter, so he could only be charged if the Queen pressed charges, and he was eventually only convicted of theft (stealing a bottle of Prince Charles' wine). He also spent three months in a psychiatric

Queen Elizabeth II waving to crowds in Queensland, Australia

hospital, and his remarkable exploits were later used as the basis for an episode of 'The Crown'.

September 29th: Tylenol Murders In Chicago

From the early hours of September 29th, seven people died after taking the paracetamol-based painkiller Tylenol. Mary Kellerman was the first confirmed fatality (09:56) when she passed away at the Alexian Brothers Medical Center (Elk Grove Village) around three hours after taking the medication. At noon, Adam Janus took two Tylenol and collapsed shortly after; he died around 15:15 at the Northwest Community Hospital. Mary "Lynn" Reiner also took some

Tylenol at approximately 15:45 due to feeling unwell and was rushed to Winfield's Central DuPage Hospital. The Janus family had returned to Adam Janus' home, and while there, his younger brother Stanley and wife Theresa took two Tylenol pills. They also collapsed and were rushed back to Northwest

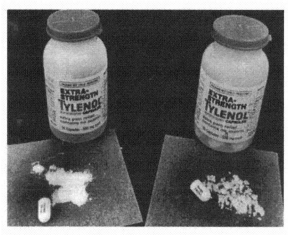

5 deaths tied to pills

Fear killer put cyanide in Tylenol

The front page of the Chicago Tribune on Oct. 1, 1982

Community Hospital. At this point, the medical staff realized something systematic was happening. They called in public health officials and the Elmhurst Police Department. At 18:30, Mary McFarland took at least one Tylenol while she was at work and was found on the floor several minutes later. During the investigation at the Janus residence, one of the investigators eventually suspected that what linked the sudden illness of the three family members was a Tylenol bottle. Stanley Janus was then pronounced dead at 20:15. Around 22:00, investigators had two different Tylenol bottles from two crime scenes, saw they were the

The Tylenol Pills

same control number and noticed a smell of almonds. At this stage, the cause of death was suspected to be cyanide ingestion. At 03:15 on September 30th, McFarland was pronounced dead at the Good Samaritan Hospital, and at 09:30, Reiner died at Central DuPage Hospital. Johnson & Johnson announced a recall of all Tylenol that was issued under control # MC2800. Northwest Community Hospital took Theresa Janus off life support at 13:15 on October 1st, and the body of Paula Prince was discovered at 17:00 in her apartment; she had purchased Tylenol on September 29th as she returned home from work. James William Lewis sent an extortion letter to J&J that demanded $1 million to stop the poisoning. He was convicted of extortion and sentenced to 20 years, eventually serving 13, but was never tied to the cyanide murders. The person responsible for the poisoning was never caught.

Mary Kellerman   Adam Janus   Mary Reiner   Mary McFarland   Stanley & Theresa Janus   Paula Jean Prince

The victims of the murder

December 12th: Largest Cash Robbery In U.S. History

Just before midnight on December 12th, two men wearing ski masks cut a hole through the roof of the building that was used as the main headquarters of Sentry, an armoured car courier company based in the Bronx, New York. The two men, who were armed with a shotgun, were able to break into the main security office and overpower the lone guard. They handcuffed 25-year-old Christos Potamitis to a railing, and then cracked open the money room using bolt cutters and a crowbar. The two robbers made off with around $11 million, which made it the largest cash robbery in U.S. history. Other reports have suggested it was $8 million. The authorities became suspicious that it was an inside job due to

A Drawing of the Cash Robbery of 1982

the robbers' knowledge of the building and security measures, and the F.B.I. claimed jurisdiction because some of the money was federally insured. The F.B.I. set up a team to investigate the crime, and Potamitis and Eddie Argitakos were eventually convicted of theft in

A Drawing of the Cash Robbery of 1982

January 1984; both were jailed for 15 years. Steve Argitakos, father of Eddie, was also given a four-year sentence for hiding stolen money. On March 7th, 1985, two other men were also convicted in relation to the robbery. Nicholas Gregory, who was accused of being the robbery mastermind, was found guilty of several charges and given an 18-year term, while Gerassimos "Captain Mike" Vinieris, who was convicted of multiple charges, was sentenced to 15 years. Potamitis spent nine years in jail. However, he more recently co-produced the film 'Empire State', which featured Liam Hemsworth and Dwayne Johnson, and was based on the robbery.

Chapter Three: Entertainment 1982

Silver Screen

<u>'E.T. The Extra Terrestrial'</u>

It would not be an over-exaggeration to state that 1982 was a massive year for entertainment with two releases, in particular, delivering (at the time) unheard-of figures when it came to sales and returns. The first of those was the box office smash of the year - 'E.T. The Extra Terrestrial'. Released on June 11th, Steven Spielberg's family Sci-Fi movie delighted audiences across the globe, and it went on to be not only the biggest box office film of the year but also the highest-grossing film of all time (back then). It surpassed 'Star Wars' which had set the benchmark in 1977,

E.T. The Extra-terrestrial,
Steven Spielberg

but has since been surpassed by 'Jurassic Park' (1993), 'Titanic' (1997), 'Avatar' (2009), and 'Avengers: End Game' (2019). There are always caveats with records that span such a vast length of time, such as inflation, cost of living, and societal changes, but 'E.T. The Extra Terrestrial' will always be able to lay claim to being the most successful movie of its time.

When talking about cinema in 1982, it can be easy to get overawed by the humongous success of 'E.T.' but there were other very successful and still-popular films also released in 1982. Depending on what figures you are viewing, the rankings under 'E.T.' do vary. It is also worth remembering that back in 1982, films released in North America didn't reach territories like the U.K. for several months; for example, 'E.T.' was released in North America on June 11th, but it didn't appear in the U.K. until December 9th. Therefore, the most reliable data to review 1982 is domestic in-year figures such as those provided by TheNumbers.com.

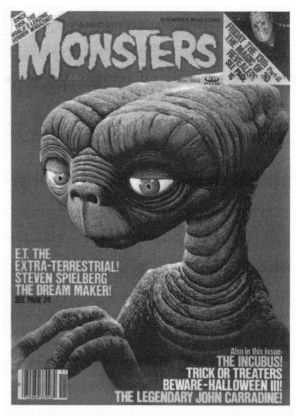

Front Cover of Famous Monsters #189, (1982)

Remaining Top Three Films

Released on December 17th, the romantic comedy 'Tootsie' sees Dustin Hoffman's character, Michael Dorsey, opting for a wig, dresses, and glasses to become Dorothy Michaels as he struggles to find acting work.

Directed by Sydney Pollack and co-starring Jessica Lange, the film went on to be the second highest-grossing film of

Tootsie (1982)

1982. Taking the bronze medal was the still-popular, uplifting romantic classic 'An Officer and A Gentleman'. It was released on August 13th, and starred Richard Gere as Zack Mayo and Debra Winger as Paula Pokrifki. Louis Gossett, Jr. went on to win Best Supporting Actor in 1983 for his portrayal of Sgt. Emil Foley, while the song 'Up Where We Belong' (Joe Cocker/Jennifer Warnes) won the Oscar for Best Music (Original Song) in 1983, plus a Golden Globe, a Grammy, a B.A.F.T.A. and a U.S. Number 1.

Richard Gere and Debra Winger in An Officer and a Gentleman (1982)

Other Top Ten Films

Two extremely successful franchises also had hits in 1982. Just missing out on the Top 3 was Sylvester Stallone's return as Rocky Balboa in 'Rocky III'. Also written and directed by Stallone, it came out on May 28th and was the first major movie to feature Mr. T. Much like 'An Officer...', 'Rocky III' also featured a song that would go down in history as intrinsically linked to the film - Survivor's 'Eye Of The Tiger'. The song went to Number 1 in both the U.S. and the U.K. and was one of the biggest hits of 1982.

Sylvester Stallone in Rocky III (1982)

The other popular franchise to make the Top Ten in 1982 was 'Star Trek'. Following the cerebral but rather solemn and slow-burning 'Star Trek: The Motion Picture' in 1979, the film franchise aspect of the original crew really took off in 1982 with the blockbuster 'Star Trek II: The Wrath Of Khan'. With a faster pace, vastly more action, and plenty of excitement, plus a plot that linked back to a popular 'Star Trek: The Original Series' episode, the film was considerably

Star trek II the wrath of Khan, Nicholas Meyer

more successful than its predecessor. It also foretold the future by being the first feature film to contain a completely computer-generated cinematic image sequence (the terraforming sequence that was created by Lucasfilm's Industrial Light And Magic).

Box Office Figures

TheNumbers.com Top 1982 Movies at The Domestic Box Office

Rank	Movie	Total Gross	Open Wkd Gross
1	E.T. The Extra-Terrestrial	$435,110,554	$11,911,430
2	Tootsie	$177,200,000	$5,540,470
3	An Officer and A Gentleman	$129,795,554	$3,304,679
4	Rocky III	$125,049,125	$16,015,408
5	Porky's	$109,492,484	$7,623,988
6	Star Trek II: The Wrath of Khan	$78,912,963	$14,347,221
7	48 Hrs	$75,936,265	$4,369,868
8	Poltergeist	$74,706,019	$6,896,612
9	The Best Little Whorehouse in Texas	$69,701,637	$11,874,268
10	Annie	$57,059,003	$510,632

TheNumbers.com Top 1982 Movies at The Worldwide Box Office

Rank	Movie	Total Gross
1	E.T. The Extra-Terrestrial	$792,962,972
2.	Tootsie	$177,200,000
3.	An Officer and A Gentleman	$129,795,554
4.	Gandhi	$127,767,889

5.	First Blood	$125,212,904
6.	Rocky III	$125,053,490
7.	Poltergeist	$121,706,019
8.	Porky's	$109,492,484
9.	Star Trek II: The Wrath of Khan	$95,800,000
10.	Das Boot	$84,970,337

Other Film Releases: Comedy/Fantasy/Drama

Films don't always need to smash box office records or make millions at the box office to eventually become popular or even cult classics. 1982 has its fair share of films that initially went under the radar, be it for poor reviews or lack of awareness.

In the comedy genre, there was Carl Reiner's Neo-Noir Comedy 'Dead Men Don't Wear Plaid' (May 21st), a homage to pulp detective films, starring Steve Martin.

Dead Men Don't Wear Plaid (1982)

Richard Pryor: Live On the Sunset Strip (1982)

There was 'Richard Pryor: Live On the Sunset Strip' (March 12th), which became his most lucrative stand-up movie. There were a couple of notable Fantasy releases, including 'Conan The Barbarian' (May 14th), the violent sword and sorcery movie that gave Arnold Schwarzenegger his big breakthrough.

The Dark Crystal (1982)

At the other end of the scale was the puppet-filled Fantasy movie 'The Dark Crystal' (December 17th); directed by Jim Henson and Frank Oz, it featured ground breaking animatronics, and, although it was technically a family movie, it had moments that were more adult than other work from the well-known pair.

The Sword and the Sorcerer (1982)

One of the most profitable independent films that went on to to become a cult classic was the quite violent 'The Sword and The Sorcerer' (April 23rd), another S&S Fantasy movie featuring Lee Horsley (Prince Talon), Simon MacCorkindale (Prince Mikah) and Richard Lynch (Titus Cromwell), plus a rather unique three-bladed sword. The drama film 'Sophie's Choice' (December 10th), starring Meryl Streep (Zofia Zawistowski) and Kevin Kline (Nathan Landau), was a critical and box office success; the film was nominated for countless awards and won several, of which Streep won an Oscar, a Golden Globe, and a B.A.F.T.A. for Best Actress.

Other Film Releases 1982: Sci-Fi/Horror

Both Sci-Fi and Horror had 1982 releases that are nowadays considered cult classics and possibly some of the finest in their genres.

Blade Runner Poster (1982)

One of the most important Sci-Fi titles from 1982 was Ridley Scott's 'Blade Runner' (June 25th), which featured Harrison Ford (Rick Deckard), Rutger Hauer (Roy Batty), Sean Young (Rachael), Daryl Hannah (Pris), and Edward James Olmos (Gaff). Although not initially as successful as other 1982 Sci-Fi films (i.e. 'E.T.'), the dystopian movie is now considered one of the greatest Sci-Fi films ever made.

Tron Film Poster, 1982

Another name that is instantly familiar to Sci-Fi fans will be 'Tron' (July 9th). Starring Jeff Bridges (Kevin Flynn), Bruce Boxleitner (Tron/Alan Bradley), and David Warner (Ed Dillinger/Sark), it was one of the first films to use CGI to a vast degree and, as such, is considered ground breaking.

The Thing Poster, 1982

One of the most important Horror releases of the year was John Carpenter's 'The Thing' (June 25th). A remake of 'The Thing from Another World' (1951), the film's initial reviews were very negative, but it has gone on to be regarded as one of the ten greatest ever Horror movies ever made in numerous rankings. The claustrophobic backdrop and never-ending paranoia have turned it into a cult classic that is loved by many, and it's now considered a milestone film. Kurt Russell (R.J. MacReady) and Keith David (Childs) turn in strong performances, and Carpenter's direction was of its usual high standard. The real star of the movie, however, was unquestionably the special effects that are equally gut-wrenching and horrific as they were technically impressive given no CGI was involved; they still stand the test of time to this day.

Award Winners

The 39th Golden Globe Awards - Saturday, January 30th, 1982: Beverly Hilton Hotel, Beverly Hills, Los Angeles, CA.

39th Annual Golden Globe Awards (TV Special 1982)

Winners

Best Picture Drama (Film)
– On Golden Pond

Best Picture Musical/Comedy (Film)
– Arthur

Best Actress Motion Picture Drama -
Meryl Streep (The French
Lieutenant's Woman)

Best Actor Motion Picture Drama -
Henry Fonda (On Golden Pond)

Best Actress Motion Picture
Musical/Comedy - Bernadette Peters
(Pennies From Heaven)

Best Actor Motion Picture
Musical/Comedy - Dudley Moore
(Arthur)

Best Supporting Actress Motion
Picture - Joan Hackett
(Only When I Laugh)

Best Supporting Actor Motion
Picture - John Gielgud (Arthur)

Best Director Motion Picture -
Warren Beatty (Reds)

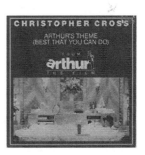

Best Motion Picture Song - Arthur's
Theme (Best That You Can Be)
(Arthur)

The 35th British Academy Of Film And Television Arts Awards - Thursday, March 18th, 1982.

Winners

Best Actor (Film) - Burt Lancaster
(Atlantic City)

Best Supporting Artist (Film) -
Ian Holm (Chariots Of Fire)

Best Actress (Film) - Meryl Streep
(The French Lieutenant's Woman)

Best Director (Film) - Louis Malle
(Atlantic City)

Best Original Music (Film) -
The French Lieutenant's Woman
(Carl Davis)

Best Film - Chariots Of Fire
(David Puttnam)

The 54th Academy Awards - Monday, March 29th, 1982: Dorothy Chandler Pavilion, Los Angeles Music Center, Los Angeles, CA.

The 54th Academy Awards Ceremony Poster

Winners

Best Actor in a Leading Role - Henry
Fonda (On Golden Pond)

Best Actor in a Supporting Role -
John Gielgud (Arthur)

Best Actress in a Leading Role -
Katharine Hepburn
(On Golden Pond)

Best Actress in a Supporting Role -
Maureen Stapleton (Reds)

Best Director - Warren Beatty (Reds)

Best Music (Original Score) -
Chariots Of Fire (Vangelis)

Best Music (Original Song) -
Arthur's Theme
(Best That You Can Do)

Best Picture - Chariots Of Fire
(David Puttnam, Producer)

Top Of The Charts

Michael Jackson - 'Thriller'

As far as studio albums go, and any albums for that matter, 'Thriller' was an absolute behemoth. The album was released on November 30th and quickly became the greatest selling album of all time. In terms of sales, widely different figures have been suggested, from 40 million right up to 150 million. On May 11th, 2017, the Guinness Book Of World Records

Thriller by Michael Jackson, 1982

recognized 'Thriller' as the Best-Selling Album with 66 million units sold (GuinnessWorldRecords.com). At one time, it was both the top-selling album in America and worldwide, but it has since been passed in the United States by the Eagles' 'Their Greatest Hits (1971-1975). In 2021, 'Thriller' was awarded 34x multi-platinum by the Recording Industry Association of America with 34 million sales, whereas the Eagles' compilation sits atop the pile with 38 million sales (Statista-September 2020).

In January 2020, AllTopEverything.com listed the three best-selling albums in history as Michael Jackson: 'Thriller' (67 million), AC/DC: 'Back In Black' (51.2 million), and Pink Floyd: 'The Dark Side Of The Moon' (46.1 million).

Debates about actual sales figures aside, there is no doubting that 'Thriller' was an extraordinary commercial and artistic achievement. However, it wasn't just about the seven Top 10 hit singles or album sales. Jackson also released three videos, and while the videos for 'Billie Jean' and 'Beat It' were memorable, they paled into insignificance when compared to Jackson's effort for 'Thriller'. Written and directed by John Landis, the 14-minute video is every bit as iconic as the album itself, if only for the choreographed dancing and Jackson being turned into a werewolf. It was only fitting that the world's best-selling album should have a music video of equal stature and standing.

Michael Jackson, 'Thriller' Halloween Flash Mob 1982

Best Albums And Singles

Although it is easy to obtain lists of best-selling albums for the U.S., the U.K., and worldwide, it is difficult to ascertain how accurate those lists are because actual album sales were recorded differently. Sometimes, they were even estimated based on airplay and a cross-section of sales. The best way to ascertain the best-selling albums and singles worldwide from 1982 is to combine their success and performance across multiple charts. One such website, TSort.info, has done just that, and provides a comprehensive selection of information from a vast collection of singles and album charts around the world.

Top Albums Of 1982

1. Michael Jackson - 'Thriller'
2. Paul McCartney - 'Tug Of War'
3. Men At Work - 'Business As Usual'
4. Asia - 'Asia'
5. Roxy Music - 'Avalon'
6. Toto - 'Toto IV'
7. Dire Straits - 'Love Over Gold'
8. Simon & Garfunkel - 'The Concert In Central Park'
9. Prince - '1999'
10. John Cougar Mellencamp - 'American Fool'

Michael Jackson, 'Thriller' Album Cover 1982

Top Singles Of 1982

1. Survivor - 'Eye Of The Tiger'
2. Joan Jett & The Blackhearts - 'I Love Rock 'N' Roll'
3. Culture Club - 'Do You Really Want To Hurt Me?'
4. Paul McCartney & Stevie Wonder - 'Ebony & Ivory'
5. The Human League - 'Don't You Want Me?'
6. Steve Miller Band - 'Abracadabra'
7. J Geils Band - 'Centrefold'

Eye of the Tiger, Album Cover 1982

8. Men At Work - 'Down Under'
9. Dexys Midnight Runners - 'Come On Eileen'
10. F R David - 'Words'

Award Winners

The 24th Annual Grammy Awards - Wednesday, February 24th, 1982: Shrine Auditorium, Los Angeles, CA.

24th Annual Grammy Awards Poster

Winners

Record Of The Year - Bette Davis Eyes (Kim Carnes)

Album Of The Year - Double Fantasy (John Lennon & Yoko Ono)

Song Of The Year - Bette Davis Eyes (Kim Carnes)

Best New Artist - Sheena Easton

Best Album Of Original Score Music - Raiders Of The Lost Ark (John Williams)

Video Of The Year - Michael Nesmith In Elephant Parts (Michael Nesmith)

Producer Of The Year (Non-Classical) - Quincy Jones

The 2nd Brit Awards - Thursday, February 4th, 1982: Grosvenor House Hotel, London.

Winners

Best British Album - Kings Of The Wild Frontier (Adam And The Ants)

Best British Single - Tainted Love (Soft Cell)

Brit Awards Logo Poster

Best British Female - Randy Crawford

Best British Group - The Police

Best British Male - Cliff Richard

Best British Newcomer - The Human League

Best British Producer - Martin Rushent

Outstanding Contribution - John Lennon

Television

Television was very different in the early 1980s, especially in the United Kingdom, where there were only three channels (BBC1, BBC2, I.T.V.), and that situation lasted until November 2nd, when Channel 4 began broadcasting. Compare this with over a thousand commercial stations in the United States. Looking back at 1982, what stands out is how instantly recognizable so many of the names are today, be it for people in the U.S. or around the world.

Sitting at Number 1 on the Top-Rated U.S. Shows in 1982-83 is '60 Minutes', a news-related show that has been around since 1968, but below that are a number of television shows that were equally loved on both sides of the Atlantic. Taking up two spots inside the Top 5 (1982-83) are two of the

60 Minutes Poster

biggest ever soap operas - 'Dallas' and 'Dynasty' - both of which were widely watched in both the U.S. and Britain. The U.S. TV ratings cover the TV Schedule Year, which typically ran from September through to August, so the ratings for 1981-1982 need to be mentioned as well, and that year it was a reverse with 'Dallas' at Number 1 and '60 Minutes' in second place.

Looking down the Top 30 TV Shows for each year reveals a treasure trove of titles that will be remembered fondly by those who were born in the mid-Seventies and earlier. In 1981-82, other shows in the list included 'The Dukes Of Hazzard', 'Falcon Crest', 'The Love Boat' and 'Little House On The Prairie'. The list for 1982-93 has names that will be even more memorable, such as 'Happy Days', 'Hill Street

Blues', 'Knots Landing' (the 'Dallas' spin-off), 'Hart To Hart', 'The Fall Guy', and 'Magnum P.I.'

What is even more impressive is the list of new series that premiered in the 1982-83 season, many of which went on to become house-hold names in the U.S. and some of the most popular and familiar worldwide shows of their time. This collection of new series encompasses such mighty names as 'Fame' (Jan 7th), 'T.J. Hooker' (March 13th), 'Cagney & Lacey' (March 25th), 'Family Ties' (September 22nd), 'Knight Rider' (September 26th), 'Cheers' (September 30th), 'Remington Steele' (October 10th), and 'St. Elsewhere' (October 26th). One show that first aired in 1982 is effectively still running today, although in a different guise; the first episode of 'The Late Show With David Letterman' aired on February 1st and featured Bill Murray. When Letterman left, the program continued with Conan O'Brien, Jimmy Fallon, and, most recently, Seth Meyers. Even Britain had a number of shows first broadcast in 1982 that went on to become fan favorites. These include 'Countdown' and 'Brookside' (both November 2nd to open Channel 4's broadcasting), 'The Young Ones' (November 9th), and 'Allo, Allo!' (December 30th).

Television Ratings (Classic-TV-Database.com)

1981-82 Shows	Est. Audience
1. 'Dallas'	23,146,000
2. '60 Minutes'	22,575,500
3. 'The Jeffersons'	19,071,000
4. 'Three's Company	18,989,500
5. 'Alice'	18,500,500
6. 'The Dukes Of Hazzard'	18,419,000
7. 'Too Close For Comfort'	18,419,000
8. 'A.B.C. Mon. Night Movie'	18,337,500

9. 'M*A*S*H'	18,174,500
10. 'One Day At A Time'	17,930,000

1982-83 Shows	Est. Audience
1. '60 Minutes'	21,241,500
2. 'Dallas'	20,491,800
3. 'M*A*S*H'	18,825,800
4. 'Magnum P.I.'	18,825,800
5. 'Dynasty'	18,659,200
6. 'Three's Company'	17,659,600
7. 'Simon & Simon'	17,493,000
8. 'Falcon Crest'	17,243,100
9. 'The Love Boat'	16,909,900
10. 'The A-Team'	16,743,300

Award Winners

The 39th Golden Globe Awards - Saturday, January 30th, 1982: Beverly Hilton Hotel, Beverly Hills, Los Angeles, CA.

Winners:

Best Drama Series - Hill Street Blues

Best Musical/Comedy Series - M*A*S*H

Best Television Motion Picture - Bill

Producers of "Hill Street Blues" pose together after receiving an award on Golden Globe Awards

Best Actress Television Motion Picture - Jane Seymour (East Of Eden)

Best Actor Television Motion Picture - Mickey Rooney (Bill)

Best Television Actress Drama Series - A Tie Between Linda Evans (Dynasty 1981-1989) and Barbara Bel Geddes (Dallas)

Best Television Actor Drama Series - Daniel J. Travanti (Hill Street Blues)

Best Television Actress Musical/Comedy Series - Eileen Brennan (Private Benjamin TV Show)

Best Television Actor Musical/Comedy Series - Alan Alda (M*A*S*H TV Show)

Best Supporting Actress Television - Valerie Bertinelli (One Day At A Time)

Best Supporting Actor Television - John Hillerman (Magnum P.I.)

The 35th British Academy Of Film And Television Arts Awards - Thursday, March 18th, 1982.

<u>Winners</u>

Best Actor (Television) - Anthony Andrews (Brideshead Revisited)

Best Actress (Television) - Judi Dench (Going Gently, A Fine Romance, The Cherry Orchard)

BAFTA Award Trophy

Best Television Comedy Series - Yes, Minister (Peter Whitmore)

Best Television Drama Series Or Serial - Brideshead Revisited (Derek Granger, Charles Sturridge, Michael Lindsay-Hogg)

Best Television Light Entertainment Performance - Nigel Hawthorne (Yes, Minister)

Best Television Light Entertainment Programme - The Stanley Baxter Series (David Bell, John Kaye Cooper)

Best Television Original Music - George Fenton (Bergerac, Going Gently/The History Man, BBC News Theme)

The 34th Primetime Emmy Awards - Sunday, September 19th, 1982: Pasadena Civic Auditorium, Pasadena, CA.

Winners

Outstanding Comedy Series - Barney Miller

Outstanding Lead Actor in a Comedy Series - Alan Alda (M*A*S*H)

Outstanding Lead Actress in a Comedy Series - Carol Kane (Taxi)

Outstanding Directing in a Comedy Series - Alan Rafkin (One Day At A Time)

Outstanding Drama Series - Hill Street Blues

Outstanding Lead Actor in a Drama Series - Daniel J. Travanti

Outstanding Lead Actress in a Drama Series - Michael Learned (Nurse)

The 34th Annual Primetime Emmy Awards
Poster

Outstanding Supporting Actor in a Drama Series - Michael Conrad (Hill Street Blues)

Outstanding Supporting Actress in a Drama Series - Nancy Marchand (Lou Grant)

Outstanding Directing in a Drama Series - Harry Harris (Fame)

Outstanding Supporting Actor in a Comedy, Variety, Or Music Series - Christopher Lloyd (Taxi)

Outstanding Supporting Actress in a Comedy, Variety, Or Music Series - Loretta Swit (M*A*S*H)

Chapter Four: Sports Review 1982

American Sports

<u>January 24th: National Football League Super Bowl XVI 1982 (Pontiac Silverdome)</u>

The climax to the 1981-82 season was Super Bowl XVI between the San Francisco 49ers and the Cincinnati Bengals. Led by future Hall Of Fame QB Joe Montana, the 49ers jumped out to a 20-0 advantage at halftime with

San Francisco 49ers 26 vs. Cincinnati Bengals
Super Bowl XVI

touchdowns from Montana (Q1: 1-yard run) and FB Earl Cooper (Q2: 11-yard reception) and two Ray Wersching field goals (Q2: 22-yards, 26-yards). The Bengals came back in the second half with touchdowns from QB Ken Anderson (Q3: 5-yard run) and TE Dan Ross (Q4: 4-yard reception), but the 49ers extended their total to 26 with two more Wersching field goals (Q4: 40-yards, 23-yards). With 20 seconds left, the Bengals scored again (Ross 3-yard reception) to close the gap to 26-21, but the onside kick failed and the 49ers won the Super Bowl with Montana winning the M.V.P. award.

<u>May 8th-May 16th: National Hockey League Stanley Cup 1982</u>

Three of the four finals in American sports during 1982 were close-run things, but N.H.L. fans were not treated to anything remotely resembling suspense. The 1982 Stanley Cup was between the New

York Islanders (54-16-10) and the Vancouver Canucks (30-33-17), which, unlike the N.F.L., was a best of seven series. The individual games for the one-sided finals played out in the following sequence:

1982 New York Islanders

05/08 VC 5-6 NYI (OT), 05/11 VC 4-6 NYI, 05/13 NYI 3-0 VC, 05/16 NYI 3-1 VC

Mike Bossy scored 7 goals for the Islanders and Denis Potvin supplied 7 assists. Thomas Gradin slotted home 3 goals and Lars Molin created 4 assists for the Canucks. The Islanders won the Stanley Cup 4-0 and Bossy was selected as M.V.P., winning the Conn Smythe Trophy.

Islanders vs. Canucks - Throwback to 1982 Stanley Cup Finals (Mike Bossy)

Other

On February 24th in Buffalo, N.Y., at the Memorial Auditorium, Wayne Gretzky scored three goals as the Edmonton Oilers beat the Buffalo Sabres 6-3. Gretzky scored a hat trick that night, but it was his first goal that gave him the magical number of 77 goals as he beat

Phil Esposito's single-season goal record of 76. Gretzky would end the season with 92 goals, and that record still stands today.

May 27th-June 8th: National Basketball Association Finals 1982

The Los Angeles Lakers and the Philadelphia 76ers were the two teams who battled it out in the 1982 N.B.A. Finals (another best of seven series). The finals reached the sixth game and the results for each game were:

05/27 LAL 124-117 PHI, 05/30 LAL 94-110 PHI, 06/01 PHI 108-129 LAL, 06/03 PHI 101-112 LAL, 06/06 LAL 102-135 PHI, 06/08 PHI 104-114 LAL

Los Angeles Lakers Michael Cooper, 1982 NBA Finals

Jamaal Wilkes and Kareem Abdul-Jabbar top-scored for the Lakers with 118 and 108 respectively, and for the 76ers, Andrew Toney and Julius Erving totaled 156 and 150 points. The Lakers won the series 4-2, and Magic Johnson was crowned the series M.V.P.

Los Angeles Lakers vs Philadelphia 76ers, 1982 NBA Finals

August 31st-September 14th: U.S. Tennis Open 1982

The 1982 U.S. Open Final was played between Jimmy Connors (U.S.) and Ivan Lendl (Czech.), with Connors winning the title 3 sets to 1 (6-3, 6-2, 4-6, 6-4). The Women's Final featured Chris Evert Lloyd (U.S.) taking on Hana Mandlikova (Czech.), and Evert Lloyd won the match 2 sets to love (6-3, 6-1).

Jimmy Connors, US Tennis Open

October 12th-October 20th: Major League Baseball World Series 1982

In baseball, the 1982 M.L.B. World Series (another best of seven games) was played between the Milwaukee Brewers and the St. Louis Cardinals. The series lasted the full seven games and the results were:

St. Louis Cardinals: Darrell Porter 1982

10/12 MB 10-0 SLC, 10/13 MB 4-5 SLT, 10/15 SLC 6-2 MB, 10/16 SLC 5-7, 10/17 SLC 4-6 MB, 10/19 MB 1-13 SLC, 10/20 MB 3-6 SLC.

Willie McGee and Lonnie Smith scored 6 runs each for the Cardinals, while Robin Yount also scored 6 for the Brewers. Pitching-wise, Bruce Sutter topped the category with 6 strikeouts for the Cardinals, and Mike Caldwell managed the same for the Brewers. The Cardinals won 4-3, and Darrell Porter (Cardinals) was named M.V.P.

British Sports

<u>January 16th-March 20th: Rugby Union Five Nations 1982</u>

England's record in the 1982 Five Nations Rugby Union Tournament was 2 wins, 1 draw, and 1 loss. They came joint second with Scotland in the table with 5 points. England's results were:

1982 Five Nations – Rugby Union

01/16 SCO 9-9 ENG, 02/06 ENG 15-16 IRE, 02/20 FRA 15-27 ENG, 03/06 ENG 17-7 WAL

The overall tournament was won by Ireland, who won 3 games and lost 1 for a winning total of 6 points.

<u>March 13th-May 27th: English Football Cups/Division One Results 1981-1982 Season</u>

The first cup game of the year was the League Cup on March 13th, and Liverpool beat Tottenham Hotspur 3-1 after extra time. The goal scorers were Steve Archibald (Tot.: 11 minutes), Ronnie Whelan

(Liv.: 87 and 111 minutes) and Ian Rush (Liv.: 119 minutes). The 1981-1982 top division of football (now the Premier League but called the First Division in 1982) was won by Liverpool (at the close of the season on May 15th)

Tottenham Hotspurs – Holders of the English Cup

with 87 points over Ipswich Town (83), Manchester United (78), Tottenham Hotspur (71), and Arsenal (71). The 1982 Football Association Cup was played over two games in 1982, and Tottenham Hotspur were again involved. Tottenham were the holders of the Cup, and they defended their title against Queens Park Rangers. The first game was played at Wembley Stadium on May 22nd, and it ended in a 1-1 draw after extra time with goals from Glenn Hoddle (Tot.: 110 minutes) and Terry Fenwick (Q.P.R.: 115 minutes). The replay took place at Wembley on May 27th, and Tottenham ran out eventual winners 1-0 with a penalty from Hoddle (Tot.: 6 minutes).

March 27th: Annual Oxford/Cambridge Boat Race 1982

The boat race in 1982 was won by Oxford in 18 minutes 21 seconds, and they won by 3 and ¼ boat lengths.

A portrayal of the legendary annual boat races of Oxford

June 21st-July 4th: Wimbledon 1982

The 1982 Wimbledon Men's Final was the longest on record at that point, with the titanic match between American Rivals Jimmy Connors and John McEnroe lasting 4 hours and 14 minutes. Connors eventually prevailed, winning 3 sets to 2 (3-6, 6-3, 6-7, 7-6, 6-4). The Women's Final featured Martina Navratilova (originally Czech but U.S. post-1981) against Chris Evert Lloyd (U.S.), which Navratilova won 2 sets to 1 (6-1, 3-6, 6-2).

Jimmy Connors holds trophy winning Wimbledon, 1982]

International Sports

January 23rd-September 25th: Formula 1 Motor Racing 1982

The 1982 Formula 1 Championship began in South Africa on January 23rd and was won by Renault's Alain Prost. There were 16 races in total, and the final meeting in Las Vegas on September 25th was won by Michele Alboreto from Tyrrell Ford.

The overall winner of the 1982 Driver Championship was Finland's Keke Rosberg (Williams Ford), who won with 44 points

The 1982 Championship Winner, Keke Rosberg

over France's Didier Pironi (39 points - Ferrari) and Britain's John Watson (39 points - McLaren Ford). Ferrari won the Constructor Championship with 74 points over McLaren Ford (69 points) and Renault (62 points).

The 1982 Formula 1 year was marred by the death of Gilles Villeneuve on May 8th during the final qualifying session for the Belgium Grand Prix at Zonder. On his last set of qualifying tires, Villeneuve hit the back of the March car driven by Jochen Mass. His Ferrari launched in the air, flipped over, and came crashing down nose-first before it disintegrated. Villeneuve was thrown from the cockpit, and the doctors fought to save his life at the racetrack. Later that night, despite the medical staff's best efforts, Villeneuve died in hospital.

May 12th: European Cup Winners' Cup 1982

The 1982 Cup Winners' Cup was held at the Estadio del Fútbol Barcelona and was played between Spain's FC Barcelona and Belgium's Standard Liège. Barcelona won the game 2-1 with the goals scored by Guy Vandersmissen (SL.: 8 minutes), Allan Simonsen (Bar.: 45 minutes) and Quini (Bar.: 63 minutes).

UEFA Cup Winners' Cup 1982

May 26th: European Cup Final 1982

The 1982 European Cup
Final (now called the
European Champions
League) took place at the
De Kuip Stadium in
Rotterdam between
England's Aston Villa and
Germany's Bayern
München. Aston Villa
won the game 1-0 with a
Peter Withe goal (67
minutes)

UEFA Winners' Cup Final 1982

June 13th-July 11th: F.I.F.A. World Cup 1982

The teams that made it through the
group stage were - Group A - Poland,
Belgium, U.S.S.R., Group B -
Germany, England, Spain, Group C -
Italy, Argentina, Brazil, Group D -
Austria, France, Northern Ireland.
The semi-finals were held on July
8th, and the results were Poland 0-2
Italy and Germany 3-3 France (after
extra time with Germany winning 5:4
on penalties). The 1982 World Cup

FIFA World Cup Spain Logo
1982

Final took place on July 11th, and Italy beat Germany 3-1 with the
goals scored by Paolo Rossi (Ita.: 57 minutes), Marco Tardelli (Ita.:
69 minutes), Alessandro Altobelli (Ita.: 81 minutes) and Paul

Breitner (Ger.: 83 minutes). The tournament's top scorer was Rossi with 6 goals.

September 30th-October 9th: XII Commonwealth Games In Australia

The 1982 Commonwealth Games featured 46 nations, 1,583 athletes, a new record at the time, and 571 officials. The medal table was won by Australia (39G, 39S, 29B - 107 overall), with England finishing second (38G, 38S, 32B - 108 overall), and Canada third (26G, 23S, 32B - 82 overall).

XII Commonwealth Games

November 26th-28th: Davis Cup Final 1982

America and France faced off against each other for the 1982 Davis Cup at the Sports Palace in Grenoble, France. The two-day final involved 5 matches; the United States won 4-1:

John McEnroe, the man who sealed a place in the Davis Cup Final

Match 1 - John McEnroe beat Yannick Noah 3-2 (12-10, 1-6, 3-6, 6-2, 6-3)

Match 2 - Gene Mayer beat Henri LeConte 3-1 (6-2, 6-2, 7-9, 6-4)

Match 3 - Peter Fleming/John McEnroe beat Henri LeConte/
Yannick Noah 3-0 (6-3, 6-4, 9-7)

Match 4 - Yannick Noah beat Gene Mayer 2-0 (6-1, 6-0)

Match 5 - John McEnroe beat Henri LeConte 2-0 (6-2, 6-3)

Chapter Five: General 1982

Pop Culture

January 20th: Ozzy Osbourne Bites A Real Bat

Heavy Metal icon and Black Sabbath frontman Ozzy Osbourne made headlines when he bit the head off a bat during a show at the Des Moines Veterans' Memorial Auditorium. Some reports state the bat was alive and others that it was dead, but the person

Ozzy Osbourne bites the head off a bat

who threw it, Mark Neal, has confirmed it was dead and was, in fact, bordering on "rancid." (DesMoinesRegister.com) Over the years, Osbourne has often spoken about that night and regularly stated that he thought it was a fake bat made of rubber. Or perhaps that was just the taste!

May 28th: Pope John Paul II Visited United Kingdom

Pope John Paul II's six-day visit to the U.K. in 1982 was the first time in over 400 years that a reigning Pope had come to Britain. During his stay, the Pope's itinerary included stops at Westminster Cathedral,

Papal visit to Britain, 1982

Southwark Cathedral, Canterbury Cathedral (where he met the

Archbishop Dr. Robert Runcie), Wembley Stadium, Crystal Palace, Coventry, Cardiff, Liverpool, Roehampton, York, Manchester, Edinburgh, and Glasgow. He also had an audience with the H.R.H Queen Elizabeth II, plus Prince Charles and Princess Diana.

September 15th: USA TODAY First Published

The first edition of USA TODAY was published in 1982, featuring a front page that contained stories about the death of Grace Kelly (Princess Of Monaco) and a Spanish plane crash with 327 survivors (55 dead).

1982 USA Today 1st newspaper issue

September 19th: First Smiley Used In An Email

```
19-Sep-82 11:44     Scott E  Fahlman              :-)
From: Scott E  Fahlman <Fahlman at Cmu-20c>

I propose that the following character sequence for joke markers:

:-)

Read it sideways.  Actually, it is probably more economical to mark
things that are NOT jokes, given current trends.  For this, use

:-(
```

Email where the first smiley was used

Professor Dr. Scott E. Fahlman from Carnegie Mellon School Of Computer Science in Pittsburgh first used a sideways "smiley" in an email and is now recognized as being the inventor of the first emoticon.

Scott Fahlman, the man who created the first emoticon

December 11th: ABBA's Last Live Performance

Although it wasn't known at the time, ABBA's performance on 'The Late, Late Breakfast Show' (a BBC live evening program hosted by Noel Edmonds) on December 11th would turn out to be the last time the Swedish quartet performed together in public (it was filmed in

ABBA in London in 1982

front of a small studio audience in Stockholm) for over 30 years. The show featured ABBA performing 'Thank You For The Music', 'Under Attack', and 'I Have A Dream.' The group eventually performed together again in 2016, and have since recorded and released a new album in late 2021 entitled 'Voyage.'

Technological Advancements

January 7th: Commodore 64 Launched

The Commodore 64 was unveiled at the Winter Consumer Electronics Show in Las Vegas. It went on sale in August 1982 for $595 and was a massive success, with sales of 17 million between 1983 and 1986. Production of the computer ended on April 29th, 1994.

The Commodore 64, bestselling computer of all time

August 17th: First CD Produced

The first compact disc for commercial release was manufactured at the Philips Langenhagen factory (which belonged to Polygram) located near Hanover in Germany. It was a pressing of ABBA's 'The Visitors'. Over the next 25 years, over 200 billion CDs would be sold.

The Visitors CD by The ABBA Group

October 1st: First CD Player And CD Album Released

There was a double first involving CDs on October 1st. Sony released the first commercially available CD player (CDP-101) in Japan. On the same day, the first album to ever be released on CD, '52nd

World's First CD Player

Street' by Billy Joel, was also made available to the public. ABBA's 'The Visitors' wasn't available for people to buy at that time. The first CD to sell 1 million copies and outperform its vinyl cousin was 'Brothers In Arms' by Dire Straits in 1985 (CNN.com).

December 2nd: First Artificial Heart Transplant

At the University Of Utah Hospital, Dentist Barney Clark was the recipient of the world's first permanent artificial heart. The surgery lasted seven hours and was conducted by Dr. William DeVries, M.D. Clark survived for 112 days, but died the following year on March 23rd, 1983.

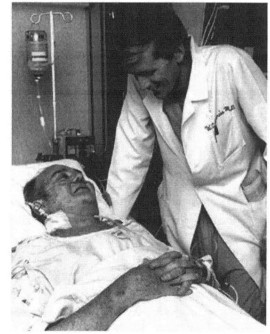

The First Artificial Heart successfully transplanted into a patient

67

Chapter Six: Births And Deaths 1982

Births (OnThisDay.com)

January 1st - David
Nalbandian: Argentine
Tennis Player

January 9th - Kate
Middleton: Duchess of
Cambridge

January 29th - Adam
Lambert: American
Singer

February 10th - Justin
Gatlin: American
Sprinter

March 2nd - Ben
Roethlisberger: American
N.F.L. Football Player

March 3rd - Jessica
Biel: American
Actress

March 4th - Landon Donovan: American Soccer Player

March 8th - Craig Stansberry: American M.L.B. Baseball Player

March 26th - Mikel Arteta: Spanish Football Player/Arsenal Manager

April 3rd - Jared Allen: American N.F.L. Football Player

April 5th - Matt Pickens: American Soccer Player

April 5th - Hayley Atwell: British Actress

April 11th - Ian Bell: English Cricketer

April 24th - Kelly Clarkson: American Singer

April 30th - Kirsten Dunst: American Actress

May 17th - Tony Parker:
French N.B.A. Basketball
Player

May 24th - Bill Haas:
American
Golfer

June 1st - Justine Henin:
Belgian Tennis
Player

June 21st - Prince
William: Duke Of
Cambridge

July 13th - Joost van den
Broek: Dutch
Keyboardist/Producer

July 13th - Yadier Molina:
Puerto Rican M.L.B.
Baseball Player

July 19th - Jared
Padalecki: American
Actor

July 30th - Jimmy/James
Anderson - England
Cricketer

July 31st - DeMarcus Ware:
American N.F.L. Football
Player

August 9th - Tyson
Gay: American
Sprinter

August 28th - LeAnn
Rimes: American
Singer

August 30th - Andy
Roddick: American Tennis
Player

September 22nd - Billie
Piper: English
Singer/Actress

September 27th - Lil
Wayne/Dwayne Michael
Carter, Jr.: American Rapper

October 2nd - Tyson
Chandler: American N.B.A.
Basketball Player

October 4th - Jered Weaver:
American M.L.B. Baseball
Player

October 7th - Jermain
Defoe: English Soccer
Player

October 13th - Ian
Thorpe: Australian
Swimmer

October 22nd - Robinson
Canó: Dominican M.L.B.
Baseball Player

October 22nd - Heath
Miller: American N.F.L.
Football Player

October 28th - Matt
Smith: English
Actor

November 4th - Devin
Hester: American N.F.L.
Football Player

November 12th - Anne
Hathaway: American
Actress

November 30th - Elisha
Cuthbert: Canadian
Actress

December 3rd - Michael
Essien: Ghanaian Soccer
Player

December 6th - Alberto
Contador: Spanish
Cyclist

December 19th - Mo
Williams: American N.B.A.
Basketball Player

Deaths (OnThisDay.com)

January 5th - Hans
Conried: American
Actor

January 8th - Rita Shaw:
American
Actress

February 17th - Thelonious
Monk: American
Musician/Composer

March 5th - John Belushi:
American Actor/
Comedian/Singer

March 19th - Randy
Rhoads: American
Guitarist

March 21st - Harry H.
Corbett: English
Actor

April 15th - Arthur
Lowe: English
Actor

May 8th - Gilles Villeneuve:
Canadian Motor Racing
Driver

May 28th - Lieutenant Colonel
Herbert Jones: British Army
Officer (VC/OBE)

June 8th - Satchel Paige:
American M.L.B. Baseball
Player

July 21st - Dave
Garroway: American
TV Host

July 22nd - Lloyd Waner:
American M.L.B. Baseball
Player

July 29th - Vladimir K.
Zworykin: Russian-
American Inventor

August 12th - Henry
Fonda: American
Actor

August 29th - Ingrid
Bergman: Swedish
Actress

September 5th - Douglas
Bader: English W.W.II R.A.F.
Pilot

September 14th - Grace Kelly:
American Actress/ Princess Of
Monaco

November 22nd - Jean Batten:
New Zealand
Pilot

December 27th - John Leonard
Swigert, Jr.: American
Astronaut

Chapter Seven: Statistics 1982

* U.S. GDP 1982 - 3.344 Trillion US$ (WorldBank.org)

* U.S. GDP 2020 - 20.953 Trillion US$ (WorldBank.org)

* U.K. GDP 1982 - 515.049 Billion US$ (WorldBank.org)

* U.K. GDP 2020 - 2.76 Trillion US$ (WorldBank.org)

* U.S. Inflation (% Change in C.P.I.) 1982 - 6.1% (GlobalEconomy.com)

* U.S. Inflation (% Change in C.P.I.) 2020 - 1.2% (GlobalEconomy.com)

* U.K. Inflation (% Change in C.P.I.) 1982 - 8.6% (GlobalEconomy.com)

* U.K. Inflation (% Change in C.P.I.) 2020 - 1% (GlobalEconomy.com)

* U.S. Population 1982 - 231,664,000 (WorldBank.org)

* U.S. Population 2020 - 329,484, 123 (WorldBank.org)

* U.K. Population 1982 - 56,313,641 (WorldBank.org)

* U.K. Population 2020 - 67,215,293 (WorldBank.org)

* U.S. Population By Gender 1982 - F: 118,069,136   M: 113,594,864 (WorldBank.org)

* U.S. Population By Gender 2020   F: 166,119,500   M: 163,034,623 (WorldBank.org)

* U.K. Population By Gender 1982 - F: 28,922,488   M: 27,391,153 (WorldBank.org)

* U.K. Population By Gender 2020 - F: 34,004, 276   M: 33,211,017 (WorldBank.org)

* U.S. Life Expectancy At Birth 1982 - 74.361 (WorldBank.org)

* U.S. Life Expectancy At Birth 2020 - 78.852 (WorldBank.org)

* U.K. Life Expectancy At Birth 1982 - 74.178 (WorldBank.org)

* U.K. Life Expectancy At Birth 2020 - 81.371 (WorldBank.org)

* U.S. Annual Working Hours Per Worker 1982 - 1,771 (OurWorldInData.org)

* U.S. Annual Working Hours Per Worker 2017 - 1,757 (OurWorldInData.org)

* U.K. Annual Working Hours Per Worker 1982 - 1,745 (OurWorldInData.org)

* U.K. Annual Working Hours Per Worker 2017 - 1,670 (OurWorldInData.org)

* U.S. Unemployment Rate 1982 - 9.708 (Index.Mundi.com)

* U.S. Unemployment Rate 2019 - 3.788 (Index.Mundi.com)

* U.K. Unemployment Rate 1982 - 10.725 (Index.Mundi.com)

* U.K. Unemployment Rate 2019 - 4.229 (Index.Mundi.com)

* U.S. Total Tax Revenue 1982 - 26.05%
  (OurWorldInData.org)

* U.S. Total Tax Revenue 2019 - 25.02%
  (OurWorldInData.org)

* U.K. Total Tax Revenue 1982 - 33.91%
  (OurWorldInData.org)

* U.K. Total Tax Revenue 2019 - 34.26%
  (OurWorldInData.org)

* U.S. Prison Population 1980 - 503,586 (PrisonStudies.org)

* U.S. Prison Population 2018 - 2,102,400 (PrisonStudies.org)

* U.K. Prison Population 1980 - 43,109 (PrisonStudies.org)

* U.K. Prison Population 2020 - 79,514 (PrisonStudies.org)

* U.S. Cost Of Living: $100 in 1982 would equate to the spending power of $294.01 in 2022. That is a total change of 194.01% in forty years (In2013Dollars.com).

* U.K. Cost Of Living: £100 in 1982 would equate to the spending power of £376.05 in 2022. That is a total change of 276.05% in forty years (In2013Dollars.com).

Cost Of Things

In 1982, the cost of various things, be it a house or a loaf of bread, was considerably different to what people would pay in 2022. Some of the prices that were charged for various items in 1982:

United States

* One Dozen Eggs - $0.87 (Stacker.com)

* One Pound Of White Bread - $0.53 (Stacker.com)

* Half-Gallon Of Fresh Milk - $1.12 (Stacker.com)

* Average Salary Per Person - $11,107 (UPI.com)

* Average Cost Of A House - $69,300 (GoBankingRates.com)

* Average Price Of A Car - $6,406 (Cheapism.com)

* Average Price Of A Gallon Of Petrol - $1.22 (Titlemax.com)

United Kingdom

* One Dozen Eggs - £0.73 (ThisIsMoney.co.uk)

* Loaf Of White Bread - £0.37 (ThisIsMoney.co.uk)

* Pink Of Milk - £0.20 (ThisIsMoney.co.uk)

* Average Salary Per Person - £7,117 (ThisIsMoney.co.uk)

* Average Cost Of A House - £23,644 (ThisIsMoney.co.uk)

* Price Of A Car (Ford Sierra/Mondeo) - £6,524 (ThisIsMoney.co.uk)

* Average Price Of A Gallon Of Petrol - £1.64 (ThisIsMoney.co.uk)

I have a gift for you!

Dear reader, thank you so much for reading my book!

In order to reduce printing costs, the images are all black & white, but I've created a special gift for you!

You can now have access, for FREE, to the PDF version of this book with the original images!

Keep in mind that some are originally black & white, but a lot of them are colored.

I hope you enjoy it!

Download it here:

https://bit.ly/3xi92OD

Or

Scan this QR Code:

I have a favor to ask you

I deeply hope you enjoyed reading this book and that you really felt transported right into 1982!

I loved researching it, organizing it, and writing it, knowing that it would make your day just a little brighter.

If you enjoyed it as well, I would be extremely grateful if you took just a few minutes to leave a positive customer review and share it with your friends. As a unknown author, that would make all the difference for me and give me all the extra energy I need to keep researching and writing and bring joy to all my readers. Thank you!

Best regards,
Duncan L. Hayward

Please leave a positive book review here:

https://amzn.to/390jWjQ

Or

Scan this QR Code:

Made in the USA
Monee, IL
11 January 2024

51563893R00052